Ceremonies and Celebrations

PILGRIMAGES AND JOURNEYS

SUE KENDALL

HODDER
Wayland

an imprint of Hodder Children's Books

Ceremonies and Celebrations

PILGRIMAGES AND JOURNEYS

Other titles in this series are:

BIRTHS • WEDDINGS • GROWING UP

LIFE'S END • FEASTS AND FASTING

Produced for Hodder Wayland by
Roger Coote Publishing, Gissing's Farm, Fressingfield
Suffolk IP21 5SH, UK

Published in Great Britain in 2001 by Hodder Wayland, an imprint of
Hodder Children's Books

© Hodder Wayland 2001

Editor: Alex Edmonds
Designer: Katrina ffiske

Consultants:
Kerena Marchant studied Theology at Bristol University. She has
worked for BBC Religious Programmes and now works for BBC
Education making media resources for primary and secondary audiences.
Marcus Braybrooke is a parish priest, lecturer and writer on interfaith
relations. He is joint President of the World Congress of Faiths.
Kanwaljit Kaur-Singh is a local authority inspector for education.
She has written many books on the Sikh tradition and appears on
television regularly.
Sharon Barron regularly visits schools to talk to children about Judaism.
She has written two books about Judaism for Hodder Wayland.
Meg St. Pierre is the Director of the Clear Vision Trust, a charitable
trust that aims to inform and educate about the teachings of the Buddha.
VP Hemant Kanitkar is a retired teacher and author of many books
on Hinduism.

Picture acknowledgements
Circa Picture Library 13, 17 (Robyn Beeche); Hutchison Library 5
(J Horner), 8 (B Regent), 25; Peter Sanders 19, 20, 21; Tony Stone
Images front cover bottom left (Nabeel Turner), 6 (Louis
Grandadam), 10 (Paul Chesley), 16 (David Sutherland); Trip front
cover top left (Dinodia), front cover top right (H Rogers), front
cover bottom right (F Good), 1 (A Tovy), 4, 7 (M Both), 9 (Z
Harasym), 11 (H Isachar), 12 (A Tovy), 14 (Dinodia), 15 (Resource
Foto), 18, 22 (Dinodia), 23 (J Sweeney), 24 (H Rogers), 26 (H
Rogers), 27 (H Rogers), 28 (H Rogers), 29 (H Rogers).

A Catalogue record for this book is available from the British Library.

ISBN 0 7502 2805 9

Printed and bound in Italy by G. Canale & C.S.p.A., Turin

Hodder Children's Books
a division of Hodder Headline Limited
338 Euston Road, London NW1 3BH

CONTENTS

What is a Pilgrimage?

People all over the world have places that are very special for them. Sometimes these are places that remind them of a particular person or event, and sometimes they are places that help them to remember why they joined the faith tradition that they follow, thereby strengthening their faith.

Millions of Muslims visit Makkah every year to make the Hajj pilgrimage. ▼

People often choose to travel to these sites because it is part of their religious tradition. Often with other followers, they journey to places of religious significance, such as shrines or holy cities.

This type of visit is sometimes called a 'pilgrimage'. Pilgrimages can be made alone or with a few friends and family, but often a large group of believers will go on a pilgrimage together. In some faiths a pilgrimage may be a once in a lifetime event, for others it may happen every year, or even more regularly than that.

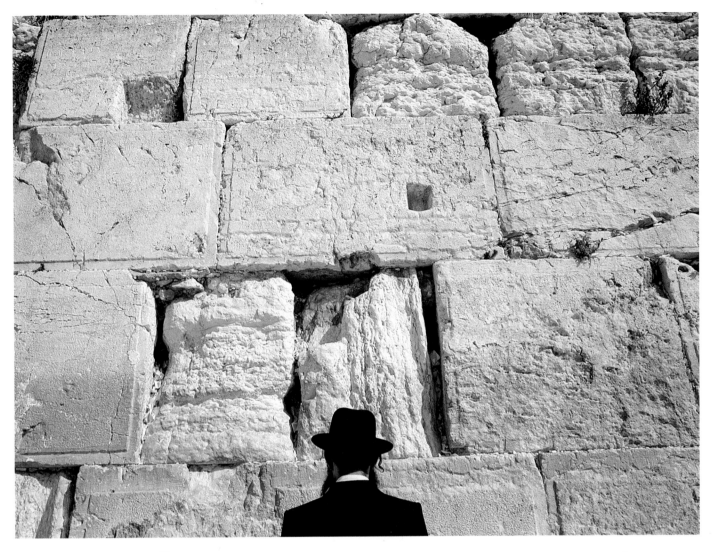

A special journey

When pilgrims arrive at the place of pilgrimage, they will often perform rituals and worship together. For many, part of the pleasure of a pilgrimage is being with people who have the same beliefs as themselves. Other people may choose to pray or meditate quietly on their own. A pilgrimage is a special time, and many pilgrims spend years saving up and preparing for pilgrimages to faraway places.

This book will introduce you to pilgrimages from the six main world religions. It will tell you about some of the journeys and pilgrimages that believers go on.

▲ *Pilgrimages can be quiet times, when a pilgrim can pray privately to God. This Jewish man is praying at the Western Wall in Jerusalem.*

The Christian Tradition

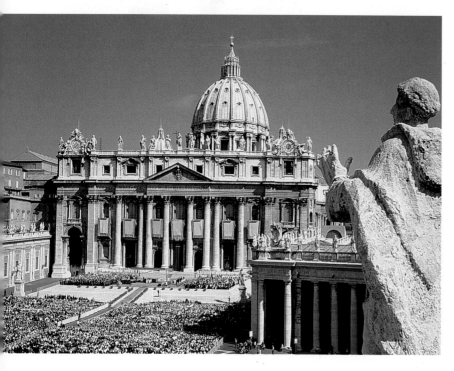

There are lots of places, all over the world, where Christians choose to go on a pilgrimage. Christians believe that God sent his son, Jesus, from heaven to Earth to teach people how to live good lives. While Jesus was on Earth he preached God's teachings to people and taught his disciples how to be true Christians. Many Christians go to visit special places which were important in Jesus' life on Earth. Others go to places where they believe miracles have happened.

▲ At special times, such as Easter, the Pope blesses crowds of pilgrims in open-air services outside the Vatican Palace.

Christians go on pilgrimages for many reasons. They go to refresh their faith, thank God for something good that has happened or ask for forgiveness if they have done something wrong. Pilgrimages can take place at any time of year, but many Christians choose to go at festival times or on the anniversary of a special event. Many believers find that being with other pilgrims helps them to think about their faith.

The Pope

Some Christians choose to visit places that have been important in the history of Christianity. Many Roman Catholic Christians make the journey to Rome, Italy, where the Pope lives. They believe he is chosen by God to lead the Church and they come to hear his teaching and prayers.

Sophie's story

'My name is Sophie. Last Easter I went with my mum on a pilgrimage to Jerusalem to see where Jesus died and rose again. It was quite warm when we got there. We went to the old city where there were thousands of people all walking very slowly behind men carrying a heavy wooden cross – just like Jesus did on his own. As we followed behind, people were praying quietly to themselves or joining in hymns. It made me feel very special to know that this is where Jesus had walked.'

▲ *These pilgrims are part of the crucifixion procession along the Via Dolorosa on Good Friday.*

The Holy Land

At some time in their lives, many Christians try to go to the Holy Land, where Jesus lived around 2,000 years ago. They can visit Bethlehem where he was born, Nazareth where he grew up and Galilee, where he told people about God's teachings. In Jerusalem, Christians can follow the route of Jesus' entry into the city on Palm Sunday. This is the route along which he was later led to his crucifixion, down the Via Dolorosa, on Good Friday. They can also see the tomb from which he rose on Easter Day. The Romans, who ruled over Israel, crucified Jesus. They were scared that the people they ruled would want Jesus as their leader rather than Roman rule.

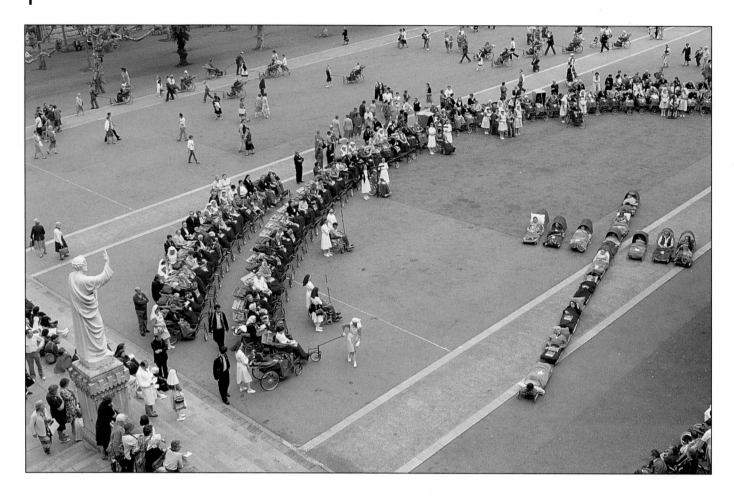

The festival of Easter is especially important for Christians. Many Christians make the journey to Jerusalem during Easter. On Good Friday many pilgrims join the procession along the Via Dolorosa and relive the events of the day on which Jesus was crucified. They pray and think about how Jesus gave his life for them.

▲ *Pilgrims join a healing ceremony at Lourdes, France, hoping to be cured of their illnesses.*

Miracles

All over the world there are sites where people believe miracles have taken place or saints have appeared. There are also places, such as Fatima in Portugal, where the Virgin Mary is said to have appeared. Very often people making journeys to these sites go to pray for people who are ill or suffering and to ask God to cure them. Many people make the journey to Lourdes in France.

It was here in 1858 that Christians believe the Virgin Mary appeared to a young girl and told her where a source of healing water was. When they are there many Christians join in healing ceremonies, or pray quietly. Others choose to collect holy water to take home, because they believe that it will bring them good fortune.

Worshippers in Poland carry a statue of the Virgin Mary, who many Christians believe appeared to three children in Fatima, Portugal in 1917. ▼

Sacred text

This text tells of Jesus and his family going on a pilgrimage to Jerusalem for Passover, and how the boy Jesus stayed behind to talk to wise men to increase his knowledge of the world.

'Now his parents went to Jerusalem every year at the feast of the Passover.
And when he was twelve years old, they went up to Jerusalem after the custom of the feast.
And when they had fulfilled the days, as they returned, the child Jesus tarried [stayed] behind in Jerusalem and Joseph [Jesus' father] and his mother knew not of it.
And it came to pass, that after three days they found him in the temple, sitting in the midst of the doctors, both hearing them and asking them questions.'

The Bible: Luke 2:41-47

The Jewish Tradition

Jews believe that about 3,000 years ago, God rescued their ancestors, who were slaves in Egypt. He chose Moses to lead them to the 'Promised Land', which is modern Israel, although at that time it was called Canaan. During the last century many Jews returned to that area and established the State of Israel. Jews believe that God gave them the Promised Land because they are his chosen people. Many Jews from different parts of the world like to visit Israel to remember the great events of their history.

This Jewish man is praying in front of the Western Wall. He is carrying a Jewish prayer book. ▼

The Western Wall

There are lots of special places in the land of Israel, which believers like to visit. Jerusalem is the ancient city that is at the heart of the religion. When they visit the city, most Jewish people like to take time to go and pray at the Western Wall. This is the last remaining part of the most famous Jewish Temple, which was destroyed in CE 70. Many worshippers gather at the Western Wall to recite the ancient traditional prayers. Men and women pray separately and some cry as they remember the history of the Jewish people. Some write special prayers on small pieces of paper and push these into the cracks between the stones of the ancient temple, hoping that their prayers will be answered.

Sacred text

This is an extract from the prayer that Jews say before going on a journey.

'May it be thy will, O Lord our God and God of our fathers, to conduct us in peace unto the haven of our desire. O deliver us from every enemy, ambush and hurt by the way, and from all afflictions that visit and trouble the world.'

From the Authorised Daily Prayer Book.

Many years ago, every Jew was expected to go to the ruins of the Temple for Pesach, Shavuot and Sukkot, and these festivals are known as the Pilgrim Festivals. Nowadays there are no fixed times when Jews should make pilgrimages, but most choose to go during the main festivals and holidays, when they can join in holiday fun with family and friends. Hasidic Jews, who follow the traditional form of Judaism, may make pilgrimages to the graves of their leaders or well-thought-of Jewish scholars.

The Holocaust

Some Jewish people also choose to make a special journey to Yad Vashem. This is the place where a memorial has been built to remember all the Jewish people who were killed or suffered during the Holocaust last century. When they visit, some people say traditional prayers or light candles, others cry as they think about what happened. Some just listen to a tape that recites the names of all the children who died in the death camps of Europe. The camps were set up by the Nazis during the Second World War to destroy the Jewish people.

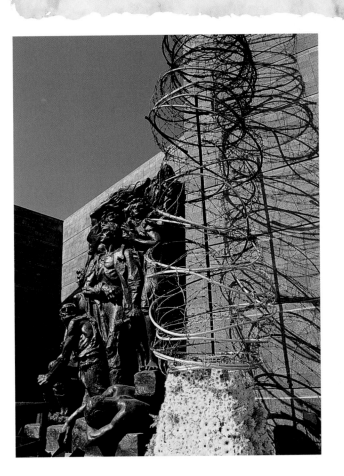

◄ This memorial at Yad Vashem in Jerusalem shows Jewish men, women and children fighting against the Nazis in Poland.

The kibbutz

Many of the ancient places that Jews choose to visit in Israel help them to remember their history. With the aim of building a stronger future for the Jewish people, Jews today often travel to a kibbutz. It has become popular for young Jewish adults to go to Israel to live and work on a kibbutz – giving up their spare time to deepen their understanding of what it means to be a Jew and learning to live as part of a community. Here they work and live together, practise their faith and try to do something to help the State of Israel. Duties include working on the land and helping with community projects.

This Jewish woman is gathering fruit as part of her daily duties as a kibbutz member. ▼

▲ *The ceremonial* Seder *plate contains symbolic foods: bitter herbs, vegetables, bitter vegetables, an apple, nut, spice and wine mixture (Charoset), shank bone (leg bone) of whatever meat the family is eating and egg.*

Passover

Even if they cannot go to Israel, many Jews around the world celebrate a special festival called Pesach or Passover. This reminds them of a very special journey that the ancient Israelites had to make to escape the persecution of the Egyptians. They celebrate by sharing a *Seder* meal together. They use symbolic foods and drink to remind them how God looked after them. They also read the story of that journey in the Bible, play games and enjoy time together as a family.

Ben's story

'My name is Ben and I am 12. I live in Leeds with my mum and dad and three sisters. Last year our family travelled to Israel. I felt very honoured that I could go to the Western Wall with dad. We said our prayers side by side, and I even wrote a prayer for my sick grandma and posted it in the wall itself. Going to Israel helped me remember our history and made me proud to be Jewish. One day I'd like to come back again!'

The Hindu Tradition

In the Hindu religion people go on many different pilgrimages and journeys. Some Hindus consider it a duty to go on a pilgrimage, or *Yatra*, as it earns special merit with the gods, good fortune and health and happiness. If they choose to make a pilgrimage, it is often to a place that has a special meaning for their chosen deity, such as Krishna or Vishnu. Different Hindu families worship different deities (gods), who are all various aspects of Brahman, the One True Spirit. There are lots of legends and stories about the lives of the deities, and some believers like to visit places where these stories took place.

These Hindus are on an annual pilgrimage to Puri, Orissa, where Lord Krishna's bones are said to have been taken when he died. ▼

▲ *This couple, in Varanasi, are taking part in a performance of the* Ramayana *story. They are dressed as the gods Rama and Sita.*

Places of pilgrimage

There are hundreds of different places that Hindus might go and visit, but there are four very famous places of pilgrimage; Varanasi where the wonderful *Ramayana* story (the Hindu epic poem about Prince Rama) is acted out for all the worshippers to see; Vrindavan which many believe was the birthplace of Lord Krishna; Rameshwaram, where the God Rama is said to have worshipped Shiva to ask forgiveness for killing someone, and Puri in Orissa, sacred to Lord Krishna (Vishnu) where many Hindus enjoy joining in as a giant statue of the God in a huge chariot is pulled through the town.

Sacred text

This text tells Hindus that they should read the sacred texts and show their devotion to God by doing godly things – such as going on pilgrimages.
'Austerity, the study of sacred texts and the dedication of action to God constitute the discipline of mystic union.'

From the *Yoga Sutra* of Patanjali

Holy rivers

Hindus have a great respect for the natural environment and often make pilgrimages to important rivers and water sources, such as the Ganges, Kaveri and Indus rivers. Many Hindu people try to visit the River Ganges in India. Bathing in its holy waters symbolizes that they are trying to lead a pure and clean life. Many confess their sins at the river. The journey is part of the pilgrimage, and some Hindus will make the travelling as difficult as they can. Some may choose to walk or crawl part of the way because they believe this proves their devotion and will find them favour with the gods.

Hindus believe in life after death. They accept that everyone is reborn in a different form, either a higher or lower life form. Because of this they believe in cremation after death. They are taught that the fire releases the human spirit to be reborn into another life. After the cremation, Hindus will often scatter the ashes of their loved one into a river, because it is a holy place.

Bathers come to Varanasi from all over India, to bathe in the holy waters of the River Ganges. This picture shows the Dasaswamedh Ghat (steps). ▼

Ashvin's story

'I am Ashvin and I am just about to turn eleven. I live in New York with my parents, two sisters and my grandmother. Last year my grandad died and we were all very sad. After he was cremated we all flew to India. We made the journey to the holy River Ganges at Varanasi where we all bathed to make ourselves clean and pure. Later my dad scattered grandad's ashes all over the water.'

Holidays and worship

Whichever site they visit, Hindus meditate and worship the gods. Sometimes they will join in singing, chanting and dancing together. Many Hindus also make offerings and light candles to show devotion to God. *Yatra* is a happy and joyful time when believers meet other Hindus and listen to the teachings of the priests. Sometimes a pilgrimage gives them the chance to visit new places, have a holiday and catch up with old friends and family members. Many choose to make a pilgrimage at a time when something important, such as a wedding or birth, is going to happen to them. They believe it brings good luck.

Pilgrims, covered in dyes that are traditionally thrown at the festival of Holi, follow the pilgrimage route at Vrindavan. Here they visit the place where they believe that Krishna was born. ▶

The Muslim Tradition

For many Muslims, the greatest way to strengthen their faith and show devotion to Allah, the One God, is a pilgrimage to the holy city of Makkah. Muslims believe it was here that the Prophet Muhammad (pbuh) received the Word of God and was instructed to teach Muslims how to lead a good life.

The Hajj pilgrimage

Muslims try to lead a sin-free life and fulfill their duties. One of these duties, the fifth of the Five Pillars of Islam (the laws that Muslims should follow), is to try to go on the *Hajj* pilgrimage at least once during their lifetime. Muslims go to Makkah because it was there that the Prophet Ibrahim (pbuh) built the *Ka'bah*, the monument to One God. The Qur'an calls all Muslims to pilgrimage

Muslim women gather at the harem (women's quarters) at the start of the Hajj *pilgrimage.* ▼

▲ *Muslims circle the Ka'bah. They believe that it contains the stone that God threw at Adam when he expelled him from Paradise for disobeying him.*

there. Every year, millions of Muslims from all over the world go on the *Hajj*. People who are sick or who cannot go, may pay for someone else to go in their place.

The *Hajj* always takes place from the 8th to the 13th day of the Islamic month of Dhul-Hijjah. Only Muslims are allowed into Makkah at any time. *Hajj* is an exciting time, but also very tiring. It is a time when all Muslims show that they are equal before God and men try to dress in the *Ihram* – simple white clothes made from two seamless pieces of cloth. These clothes represent purity, chastity and equality. Women can wear any respectable clothes.

Sacred text

This sacred text tells of how God commanded Ibrahim (pbuh) to call men to *Hajj* at Makkah.

'And proclaim unto mankind the pilgrimage. They will come unto thee on foot and on every lean camel; they will come from every deep ravine.'

Qur'an: XXII 27

Rituals of Hajj

▲ *A Muslim woman drinks from the well of Zamzam.*

Muslims show that they are all the same by performing the same rituals and actions of *Hajj* together. Many *Hajji* rituals recall the experiences of the Prophet Ibrahim (pbuh), his wife Hagar and son, Isma'il. *Hajjis* (pilgrims) walk in his family's footsteps when they are there, as a way of remembering the family's devotion to God.

Everybody circles the *Ka'bah* (a black stone structure that all Muslims must turn towards when they pray) seven times, kissing the stone, pointing at it or touching it as they start each circuit. Next the *Hajjis* run between the two hills of Safa and Marwah as Hagar, Ibrahim's wife, did in search of water. As they walk or run, they drink from the well of Zamzam where water miraculously appeared to quench Hagar's thirst. On the 9th day of the month, they travel to Mount Arafat where the Prophet Muhammad (pbuh) gave his last sermon. While here they say prayers and confess their sins. Then they travel to Muzdalifah to camp for the evening.

Here they say prayers again and read the Qur'an throughout the night. The next morning the *Hajjis* gather stones, which are taken to throw at the three pillars at Jamarat. These pillars represent Satan (the devil). On the tenth day the *Hajjis* join together for the feast of *Id-ul-Adha*. This helps them remember that Ibrahim (pbuh) was prepared to kill his son for his faith, but instead God told him to sacrifice a ram. Near the end of the pilgrimage, everyone circles the *Ka'bah* once more before changing back into ordinary clothes to travel home.

Muslims consider it a special honour to be able to join the *Hajj*. Millions of pilgrims arrive for *Hajj* from all over the world by plane and boat. Many have to save hard to make the journey, which is very tiring. They go not only because it is their duty, but also because it helps them to strengthen their faith.

Danah's story

'I am Danah and I'm 11 years old! I share a house with my parents and older brother. This year was very exciting because my brother and dad went on *Hajj* to Makkah. They told me that they would say special prayers for me and mum in Makkah. They brought us some holy water from the well of Zamzam. Dad has carefully folded the clothes he wore on *Hajj*, and says he wants to keep them forever. He also wants to make sure he is buried in them.'

◀ Hajjis *throw stones at the pillars of Jamarat.*

The Buddhist Tradition

Buddhists try to follow the teachings of the Buddha. He was a very wise teacher who lived in Nepal around BCE 560. He was born a wealthy prince, but left his luxurious lifestyle behind to find out the reasons for suffering and evil. He spent many years trying to find the answers. He eventually understood what causes suffering and how to escape from it and became the Buddha – an Enlightened being. The Buddha taught people how to live so that they could free themselves from suffering and gain Enlightenment. He taught them to follow the Eightfold Path. All Buddhists should try to develop:

▲ *This picture shows the Buddha sitting under a Bodhi tree in Bodh Gaya, where he became Enlightened.*

- Right Views, by understanding that all things change and so develop wisdom.
- Right Intention (thoughts), by committing themselves to grow and change for the better.
- Right Speech, by telling the truth and speaking in a kind and friendly way.
- Right Action, by trying not to harm living beings (steal from, kill or hurt other people or animals).
- Right Livelihood, by doing work that doesn't harm oneself or others.
- Right Effort, by trying to develop an attitude of kindness and generosity to all (following the Eightfold Path with kindness.)
- Right Mindfulness, by being aware of themselves, other people and the world around them.
- Right Concentration, by training the mind in meditation to be calm and positive in order to develop wisdom.

◄ *Pilgrims decorate the Bodhi tree that they believe Buddha sat underneath.*

The journey of life

During their lives, Buddhists try to follow this pathway and many think of it as a journey that they are on, even though they are not going to a different place! Some people may try to go and visit important places in Buddhist history. The four most popular sites are Lumbini (Nepal), where they believe Siddartha Gautama, the man who became the Buddha, was born; Bodh Gaya (India), where he achieved Nirvana or Enlightenment; Sarnath (India), where he gave his first teaching and Kushinagar (India), where he died. Pilgrims believe that visiting these special places where they believe the Buddha lived and taught helps them in their practice of Buddhism.

Sacred text

In this text, the Buddha tells his disciple, Ananda, about pilgrimages.

'Ananda, there are four places the sight of which should arouse emotion in the faithful. Which are they? "Here the Tathagata (Buddha) was born", is the first [Lumbini]. "Here the Tathagata attained supreme Enlightenment" is the second [Bodh Gaya]. "Here the Tathagata set in motion the Wheel of Dhamma" [where he gave his teachings] is the third [Sarnath]. "Here the Tathagata attained the Nibbana-element [total peace] without remainder" is the fourth [Kushinagar, where he died]. And Ananda, the faithful monks and nuns, male and female lay followers will visit those places.'

Digha Nikaya: *Maha Parinibbana Sutta*

Temples and sacred buildings

Sometimes followers cannot make the long journeys to these places, so they visit temples and *stupas* (sacred monuments) nearer to their homes. Wherever they choose to visit they pay their respects to the Buddha. Many will listen to the teachings of the monks, join in chanting and make offerings of flowers, gifts and incense. They may help redecorate the statue of the Buddha or meditate quietly under a nearby tree – just as the Buddha once did. All of these activities help them concentrate on their own journey of life, following the Eightfold Path.

These monks are praying in a park at Sarnath, where the Buddha gave his first teachings. ▼

Wesak

There is no particular time when Buddhists go on a pilgrimage, but it is good to go during a Buddhist festival when they can meet lots of other Buddhists. Visiting these places and meeting other members of the Buddhist *sangha* (community) helps them to think about the Buddha, and strengthens their resolve to follow his teachings more deeply. Lots of Buddhists like to visit special places at *Wesak*. *Wesak* is the main Buddhist festival. It is celebrated by Buddhists during the full moon in May and June. It recalls the life, birth and Enlightenment of the Buddha, and the pilgrimage sites are usually specially decorated at this time.

It is not only practising Buddhists who visit shrines and special places. Often people from other religions and traditions also like to make the same journeys. They find it helpful and restful to listen to the wise teachings from the monks and to meet and talk to Buddhists.

This stupa is in Sarnath. Here pilgrims visit the shrine to the Buddha and remember the Buddha's teachings. ▶

Ian's story

'My name is Ian. I live with my mum and dad in Holland. We are Buddhists and often go to the local temple to meet friends. Recently a group of us went to Lumbini, where the Buddha was born. There were so many people walking up the hill to the monastery. When we got there we listened to the monks' teaching and wise words. The statues of the Buddha were so beautiful and I enjoyed helping to decorate one of them. I put a large bunch of bright flowers at the Buddha's feet.'

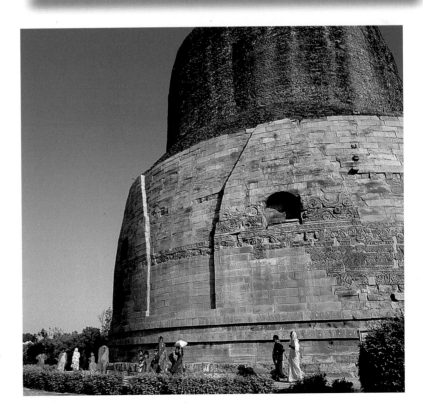

The Sikh Tradition

The Sikh religion started in the Punjab just over five hundred years ago, when Guru Nanak received a calling (he was spoken to by God) to lead his people and teach them how to follow God. The teachings do not say that believers have to go on pilgrimages to special places, but many Sikhs like to go back to the Punjab in northern India and see where the *Gurus* lived and taught. Many of them think of it as a way of showing that they are Sikhs and of strengthening their faith.

The Golden Temple

Guru Nanak was the first of the ten *Gurus*. Many of the special sites that Sikhs choose to visit are places where important events happened in the lives of the *Gurus*. Some Sikhs like to visit the Golden Temple at Amritsar because it is one of the most important sites in the faith.

The Golden Temple at Amritsar is seen as a symbol of the strength and magnificence of Sikhs all over the world. ▼

▲ *Children enjoy ritual bathing in the lake at the Golden Temple, Amritsar, India.*

Sacred text

This text from the Sikh holy book talks about how Sikhs should devote themselves to God.
'The souls on their spiritual journey chant and meditate within their minds on the One Lord, the Treasure of Excellence. The Righteous judge of Dharma serves them; blessed is the Lord who adorns them.'

From the *Guru Granth Sahib*

The fifth *Guru*, Arjan Dev, built this beautiful temple. It stands in a lake and in order to enter you have to step down into the building. This shows that you are being humble as you enter this special place. The temple has four entrances, facing in four opposite directions. This shows that Sikhs welcome everybody, from all parts of the world and they are all equal. The belief in equality is important to Sikhs.

▲ *Worshippers share the* langar *meal from leaf plates in the Golden Temple at Amritsar. This meal symbolizes the equality of all Sikhs.*

Sikh worship

When believers go into the Golden Temple, they listen to the *Guru Granth Sahib*, the holy book, being recited by the *granthi*. Some of them join in the singing. People make offerings to charity, just as they do when they worship at home. They will all join in the *langar* meal, which is provided for free to anyone visiting the temple. Twice an hour, 3,000 people eat a *langar* meal. This also shows that all Sikhs are equal because everyone shares the meal, regardless of status. Some people may then choose to bathe or wash in the holy lake around the temple.

Festival pilgrimages

Bandha's story

'My name is Bandha and I am ten years old. I live in Ireland with my grandparents, mum, dad and twin brothers. I am going to go to Amritsar this April. I am so excited because I am going to meet lots of other Sikhs from all over the world. But most of all I am looking forward to sharing the *langar* meal with thousands of people. We will all feel equal, special and very proud to be Sikh.'

There is no set time when Sikhs should go to visit these special sites, but Sikhs often go at festival times such as Baisakhi, Divali, the birthdays of Guru Nanak and Guru Har Gobind or the martyrdoms of Guru Arjan Dev and Guru Tegh Bahadur. Baisakhi is the busiest time to go, as it is the main festival. At this time, Sikhs remember the founding of the *Khalsa* by Guru Gobind Singh. On Baisakhi day, the Guru Gobind Singh asked the faithful to be prepared to lay down their lives for their faith. At Baisakhi many choose to be baptised into the faith and wear the Five Ks, the symbols of Sikhism (*Kara* – a steel bracelet; *Kirpan* – a small dagger; *Kesh* – uncut hair; *Kangha* – a comb and *Kachera* – shorts), to show that they too are Sikhs.

Going on journeys to the holy sites is very enjoyable, and is a very special time for Sikhs. It gives them the chance to share their experiences with people from all over the world and celebrate their beliefs together. It is also a private time when some choose to refresh their faith and remember the values of equality and justice which are so important to their religion.

Pilgrims place flowers on the floor of the Golden Temple. ▶

GLOSSARY

Adam the first man, created by God.

Baisakhi the Sikh festival which remembers the founding of the *Khalsa*.

CE the Christian era.

chanting rhythmic and prayerful singing.

chastity when someone decides not to have sexual intercourse, often for religious reasons.

cremation the burning of the human body after death.

crucifixion the Roman method of execution by nailing the victim to a wooden cross and letting him or her die.

deities gods or goddesses.

disciples the first twelve followers of Jesus.

Divali a festival celebrated by Sikhs to remember the release from prison of their sixth *Guru*, Guru Har Gobind. It is also celebrated as a New Year festival by Hindus.

Enlightenment to be in a state where one understands how to be free from pain and suffering.

Five Pillars of Islam the religious and moral duties of a Muslim.

granthi a Sikh leader who reads from the *Guru Granth Sahib*.

gurdwara a Sikh temple.

guru (Sikh) one of the 10 Sikh human teacher-saints. (Buddhist) a name given to a Buddhist teacher who is Enlightened.

Guru Granth Sahib the Sikh holy book.

Guru Nanak the founder of Sikhism.

Hajj the Islamic pilgrimage to Makkah.

Hasidic a very strict and pious form of Judaism, which started in the 18th century in Europe.

Holocaust the extermination of six million Jews by Nazi followers in the late 1930s and early 1940s.

Ibrahim (pbuh) (or Abraham) the Islamic prophet who taught Muslims not to worship idols.

Khalsa the Sikh community.

Krishna the Hindu god Vishnu became Krishna when he came to Earth to overcome evil.

langar a shared meal that is eaten in a Sikh *gurdwara*.

Makkah the Muslim holy city in Saudi Arabia.

martyrdom when someone suffers or is killed for his or her beliefs or faith.

meditation Buddhists meditate to remove bad thoughts from their minds. They do this in different ways – by concentrating on an image or a sound or by thinking good thoughts.

monastery a community of monks and nuns who live together and practise the Buddha's teachings.

Muhammad (pbuh) the most important prophet in Islam.

Passover the Jewish festival of Spring.

Peace Be Upon Him (pbuh) the standard phrase that is repeated after the name of an Islamic prophet as a mark of respect.

Persecution the ill-treatment of a group of people because of their beliefs, views or practices.

Pesach a festival remembering the Israelites' escape from the Egyptians.

Qur'an the Muslim holy book.

Satan the angel who was thrown out of heaven for sinning and became the enemy of God.

Shavuot the festival remembering the revelation of the holy texts, the *Torah*, on Mount Sinai.

stupas burial mounds containing important Buddhist relics.

Sukkot Jewish harvest festival.

Virgin Mary Jesus' mother.

Wesak 'Buddha day', the festival which is celebrated to remember the birth, Enlightenment and death of the Buddha.

Zamzam a sacred well in Makkah.

FURTHER INFORMATION
Books

Looking at Judaism: Special Occasions by Sharon Barron, Wayland, 1998

Easter by Catherine Chambers, Lion, 1998

Religions Through Festivals: Buddhism by Peter and Holly Connolly, Longman, 1989

Hinduism by Dilip Kadodwala, Wayland, 1995

Celebrate Hindu Festivals by Dilip Kadodwala and Paul Gateshill, Heinemann, 1995

Islam by Khadijah Knight, Wayland, 1995

Sikhism by Kanwaljit Kaur-Singh, Wayland, 1995

Islamic Festivals by Khadijah Knight, Heinemann, 1995

Id-ul-Fitr by Kerena Marchant, Wayland, 1995

Feasting for Festivals by Jan Wilson, Lion, 1990

Hinduism by V.P. (Hemant) Kanitkar, Stanley Thornes, 1989

Hinduism by V.P. (Hemant) Kanitkar and Owen Cole, Hodder and Stoughton, 1995.

Websites

http://www.theresite.org.uk – An RE site that links to resources, organizations and agencies as well and contains research materials for children.

http://www.christianity.net/ – An extensive guide with stories, a church locator, and a database of over 9,000 Christian sites.

http://www.sparksmag.com – An electronic magazine for Jewish youth, ages 9–13, with articles, interviews, polls and chat.

http://encarta.msn.com – This site contains information on Hindu beliefs, practices and pilgrimages.

http://www.hindunet.org – The Hindu Universe. This web site features a Hindu calendar, a glossary of terms and information on Hindu arts, customs, worship and scripture. Links to other Hindu resources are also included.

http://www.islam.org – IslamiCity in Cyberspace. An attractive site that explains about Islam and has a virtual mosque tour and a kids' page (http://www.islam.org/KidsCorner/Default.htm)

http://www.sikhs.org/ – An extensive range of topics, from teachings to ceremonies and festivals. Includes translated scriptures and contemporary articles.

education@clear-vision.org – The web site for the Clear Vision Trust, a project that provides Buddhist resources.

INDEX

All the numbers in **bold** refer to photographs